Disney Princess Celebrations

CELEBRATE with Tiana

Plan a *Princess and the Frog* Party

Niki Ahrens

Lerner Publications ◆ Minneapolis

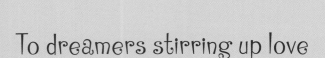

To dreamers stirring up love

Lerner Publications Company
An imprint of Lerner Publishing Group, Inc.
241 First Avenue North
Minneapolis, MN 55401 USA

For reading levels and more information, look up this title at www.lernerbooks.com.

Main body text set in Billy Infant.
Typeface provided by Sparky Type.

Library of Congress Cataloging-in-Publication Data

Names: Ahrens, Niki, 1979- author.
Title: Celebrate with Tiana : plan a princess and the frog party / Niki Ahrens.
Description: : Minneapolis : Lerner Publications, [2020] | Series: Disney princess celebrations | Includes bibliographical references and index.
Identifiers: LCCN 2019011661 (print) | LCCN 2019012984 (ebook) | ISBN 9781541582798 (eb pdf) | ISBN 9781541572720 (lib. bdg.)
Subjects: LCSH: Handicraft—Juvenile literature.
Classification: LCC TT160 (ebook) | LCC TT160 .A3326 2020 (print) | DDC 745.5—dc23

LC record available at https://lccn.loc.gov/2019011661

Manufactured in the United States of America
1-46539-47584-8/7/2019

Table of Contents

A Dreamy Party

What do you wish for? Tiana dreams big and works hard to achieve her goal. Stir up a jazzy celebration where everyone will leap for joy! You will need to do these things:

♛ Ask for an adult's permission to host your party at the right time and place. Send invitations ahead of time to gather everyone together!

♛ Prepare the party space for your guests. Add decorations, party favors, and treats.

♛ During the party, lead the activities you've created!

♛ After the fun, clean up and thank your guests.

Tips for Cooking Up Fun

- Spread newspaper over your workspace before making crafts to avoid making a mess.

- Rest well before the party.

- Wash your hands before preparing food.

- Be respectful by asking about any guests' food allergies.

- Kindly ask an adult for help using kitchen equipment.

- Warmly welcome and include every guest.

- Recycle any materials and scraps that you can.

Gumbo Pot Invitations

Tiana cooks delicious gumbo that brings everyone together. Send paper gumbo pots that invite guests to gather for festive fun.

Materials

- cardstock

- glue stick

- 2 (6-inch, or 15 cm) pieces of yarn

- pen

- scissors

- colored construction paper

1. Fold a sheet of cardstock in half.

2. Inside the card, glue both ends of a piece of yarn to one side, just under the fold. Glue a second handle to the other side.

3. Write your invitation on the inside of the card. Include the party date, time, and place!

4. Cut small, colorful vegetable shapes from construction paper.

5. Glue these vegetables onto the cover of your gumbo pot.

6. Send an invitation to each guest!

Party Tip! Did You Know?

Gumbo is a soup that combines flavors from several cultures of southern Louisiana. Common ingredients are crawfish, okra, celery, bell peppers, carrots, and onions.

Water Lily Decorations

Water lilies flicker on the tabletops in Tiana's Palace and sparkle on the swamp surface. Add their shimmer to your party.

Materials

- 5 (6-inch, or 15 cm) squares of green, white, and pink tissue paper

- scissors

- pipe cleaner

1. Stack 4 to 5 tissue paper squares together, with a green square on the bottom.

2. Accordion-fold the stack of tissue paper.

3. Cut the corners a bit to round them.

4. Wrap the center of the folded stack with a pipe cleaner.

5. Starting at the center, gently pull at the top layer of tissue paper so it stands up. Unfold the rest of the layers from the stack to make a water lily flower.

6. Make more water lilies for your splashy bayou celebration!

Beignet Bites

Tiana bakes delicious beignets that people line up to enjoy. Bake and share bite-sized versions of these sugar-dusted treats.

Materials

- butter knife
- parchment paper
- baking sheet
- basting brush
- oven mitts
- spoon

Ingredients

This recipe makes 16 to 18 bites.

- a 14-ounce (397 g) package of refrigerated biscuit or pizza crust dough
- cooking oil
- bowl of powdered sugar

1. Ask an adult to help preheat the oven to 425°F (220°C).

2. Use the butter knife to carefully cut the dough into small pieces.

3. Set 9 to 12 dough shapes apart on a parchment-lined baking sheet.

4. Gently brush a light coat of cooking oil over the dough pieces.

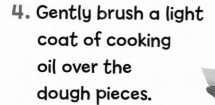

5. Ask an adult to bake the dough for 8 to 12 minutes. Then the adult will use oven mitts to remove the hot baking sheet from the oven.

6. Use a spoon to sprinkle powdered sugar on the beignet bites. Wait for the beignet bites to cool. Put the yummy treats on a pretty plate to serve your guests.

Jazz Strings

Naveen strums a ukulele with New Orleans street musicians. Your guests can find their jazzy styles on homemade ukuleles.

Materials

- scissors

- heavy-duty paper plates

- craft glue

- paint stir sticks

- assorted rubber bands

1. Cut a paper plate in half.

2. Glue the end of a paint stick to the back of the half plate to make a handle. The handle should extend from the middle of the arch.

3. Cut 4 tiny notches into the straight edge of the plate half.

4. Cut a tiny notch along the arch on either side of the paint stick.

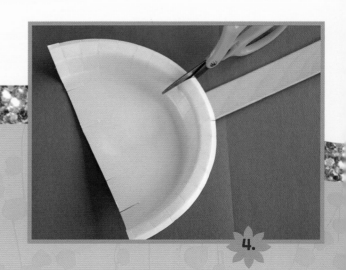

5. Stretch 4 rubber bands into the notches across the half plate.

6. Form bands and strum songs with your guests, giving each guest a chance to play solo.

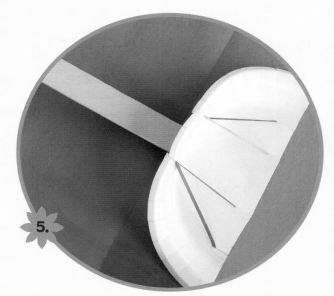

5.

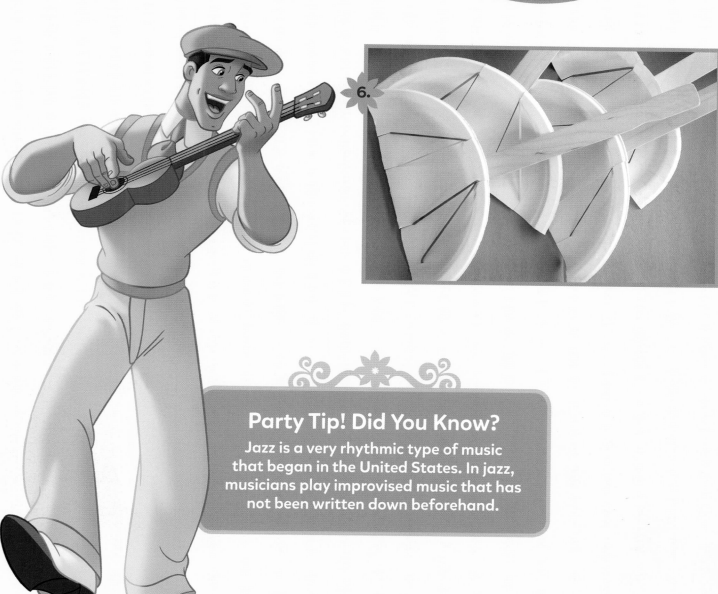

6.

Party Tip! Did You Know?
Jazz is a very rhythmic type of music that began in the United States. In jazz, musicians play improvised music that has not been written down beforehand.

Leaping Frogs

Tiana and Naveen leaped to great heights to escape frog hunters. Make lively frogs that jump into action.

Materials

- pencil
- thin paper plates
- scissors
- crayons
- craft glue
- googly eyes

1. Trace around your foot on a paper plate. Your heel can sit over the edge slightly.

2. Cut out your tracing.

3. Color the tracing with crayons, and glue googly eyes to it to make it look like a frog.

4. Fold your frog in half, keeping its eyes on top.

5. Fold the bottom of the frog into fourths, accordion style.

6. Set your frog on its folded legs. Quickly press down the back fold of the frog to cause your frog to jump.

7. Cut out tasty insects from paper plate scraps. Aim your frog at them!

Party Tip! Be Respectful
Offer to trace your friends' feet. Guests can pair up to help one another with tracing and leaping techniques.

Mardi Gras Masks Party Favors

Louis pretends he's in costume to join the Mardi Gras cheer. Give guests festive frog masks for carnival fun.

Materials

- scissors
- paper plate
- pencil
- coin
- paintbrush
- green paint
- black marker
- red scrap paper
- glue stick
- clear tape
- paper straw or craft stick

1. Cut two side-by-side semicircles into the top half of a paper plate.

2. Trace around a coin to make two eyes. Carefully poke a pencil through each traced circle. Insert the scissors into each pencil hole to cut out the traced circles.

3. Paint your mask to look like a frog.

4. Allow the paint to dry completely.

5. Use a marker to give your frog a smile.

5.

6. Cut a tongue from red paper, and glue it to your frog's smile.

7. Tape a straw or craft stick to the edge of your mask to make a handle.

6.

8. Make a festive mask for each of your guests!

7.

Twinkling Thank-You Fireflies

Ray brightens Tiana's and Naveen's time in the bayou. Send vibrant fireflies to thank your guests with friendly light.

Materials

- construction paper

- pen or marker

- scissors

- bubble packaging or plastic shopping bag

- craft glue

- craft stick

- large yellow pom-poms

- googly eyes

Party Tip! Reuse It

You can ask family or friends to help save bubble packaging for your project. When you reuse packaging instead of buying new materials, you create Earth-friendly art!

1. Fold a sheet of paper in half like a card.

2. Inside, write a happy thank-you message.

3. Cut two small, teardrop-shaped wings from used plastic packaging.

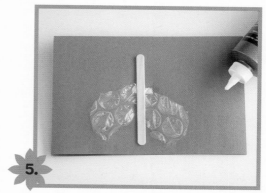

4. Glue these wings on the middle of the card's cover.

5. Glue a craft stick to the card between the wings.

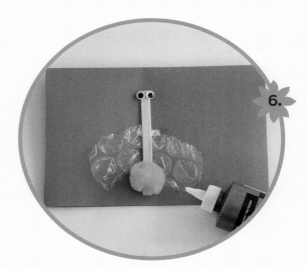

6. Glue a yellow pom-pom at the bottom of the craft stick, and glue googly eyes at the top.

7. Send a firefly flying to each guest!

Hop into Action